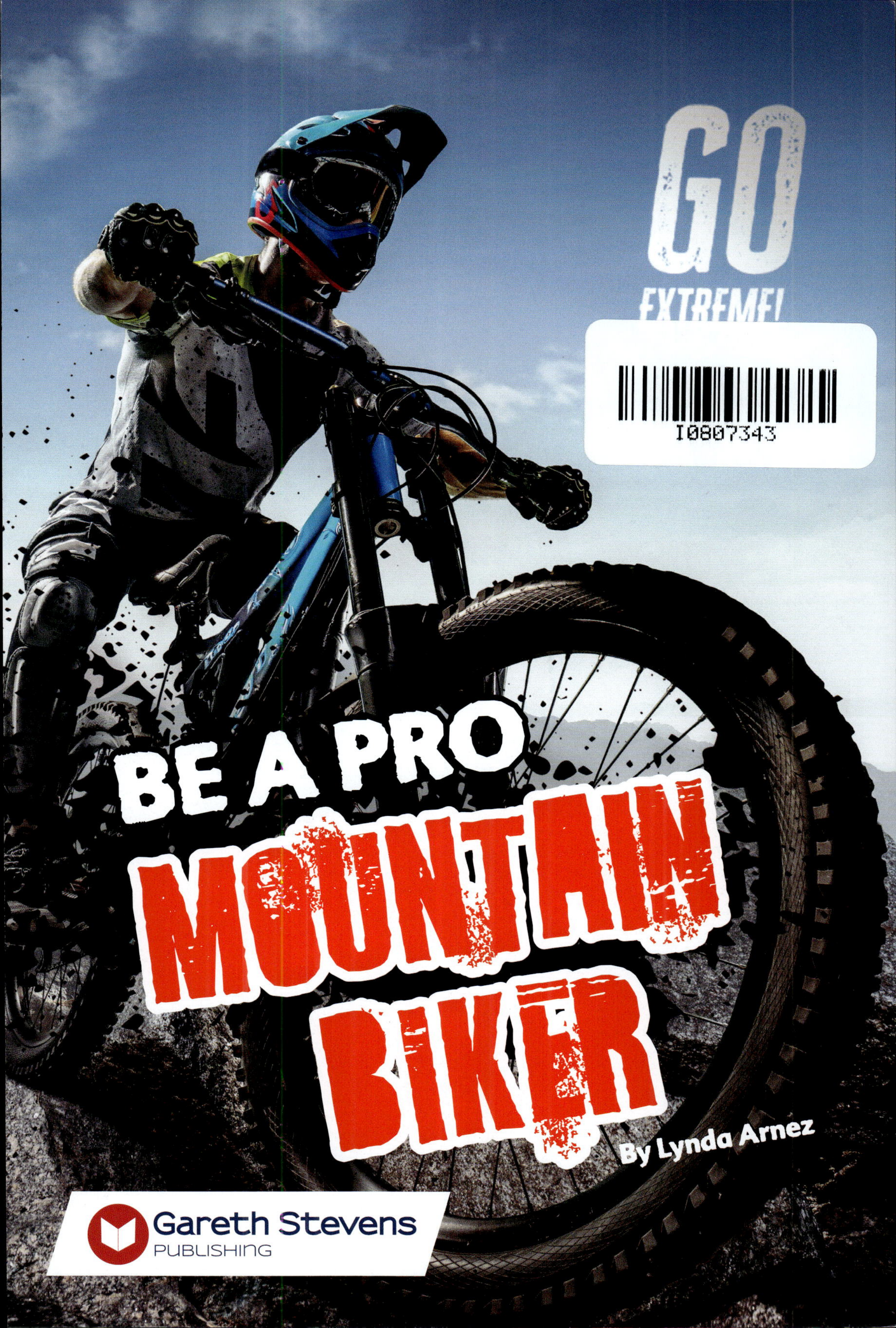

GO EXTREME!

BE A PRO MOUNTAIN BIKER

By Lynda Arnez

Gareth Stevens PUBLISHING

Please visit our website, www.garethstevens.com. For a free color catalog of all our high-quality books, call toll free 1-800-542-2595 or fax 1-877-542-2596.

Library of Congress Cataloging-in-Publication Data
Names: Arnéz, Lynda author.
Title: Be a pro mountain biker / Lynda Arnez.
Description: Buffalo, New York : Gareth Stevens Publishing, [2024] | Series: Go extreme! | Includes bibliographical references and index.
Identifiers: LCCN 2023003088 | ISBN 9781538286906 (library binding) | ISBN 9781538286890 (paperback) | ISBN 9781538286913 (ebook)
Subjects: LCSH: Mountain biking–Juvenile literature.
Classification: LCC GV1056 .A77 2024 | DDC 796.63–dc23/eng/20230126
LC record available at https://lccn.loc.gov/2023003088

First Edition

Published in 2024 by
Gareth Stevens Publishing
2544 Clinton St
Buffalo, NY 14224

Designer: Ellen Weber
Editor: Kristen Rajczak Nelson

Photo credits: Cover, p. 1 Alex Kravtsov/Shutterstock.com; series art Mind Pixell/Shutterstock.com.com; series art Duda Vasilii/Shutterstock.com; series art PegasuStudio/Shutterstock.com; series art Scott Webb/Pexels; pp. 5, 23 Monkey Business Images/Shutterstock.com; p. 7 Taras Hipp/Shutterstock.com; p. 9 yanik88/Shutterstock.com; p. 11 MikeDotta/Shutterstock.com; pp. 13, 25 martin SC photo/Shutterstock.com; p. 15 martin SC photo/Shutterstock.com; p. 17 LiveMedia/Shutterstock.com; p. 19 ingehogenbijl/Shutterstock.com; p. 21 Evgeny Bakharev/Shutterstock.com; p. 27 camoak3/Flickr; p. 29 nullplus/Shutterstock.com.

Printed in the United States of America

CONTENTS

TIME TO GET PAID!

Hitting a forest trail or mountainside on a mountain bike is a ton of fun. Now, imagine making money or getting free stuff to ride your bike. It's a dream for many that takes hard work—and maybe a little luck!

PUSHING THE LIMITS

To be a professional at a sport means getting paid to do the sport.

A LITTLE BACKGROUND

Mountain biking as it's known today started during the late 1970s in California. Today there are many types of mountain biking you can **compete** in. Downhill and cross-country are two kinds. Enduro races are named for the **endurance** you need to complete them!

PUSHING THE LIMITS

Mountain bikers may compete in many kinds of events. They often happen over a weekend or during a day-long event.

GET YOUR GEAR

The road to becoming a pro mountain biker starts with the right gear. Mountain bikes have fat tires that look knobby, or bumpy. They have **suspension** frames and flat handlebars. Mountain bikes can cost a lot of money! You don't need a fancy bike to start.

PUSHING THE LIMITS

Mountain biking is an expensive, or costly, sport. That's why going pro can seem so good!

STARTING OUT

It's time to get out there and ride! Like other sports, the more you ride your bike, the better mountain biker you'll be. Try different kinds of trails and tracks. Seek out groups in your school or community to ride with.

PUSHING THE LIMITS

Pro mountain biker Sparky Moir has said: "It's important to remember that biking is supposed to be fun. Never lose sight of it being fun."

In order to get to the pro level, you must progress, or work to get better. That means trying harder tracks and trails. It means riding for longer. Then, enter mountain biking events near you. It doesn't matter if you do well! Every time you compete, you gain **experience**.

PUSHING THE LIMITS

Speed is one area mountain bikers work on. Sometimes going fast on a mountain bike can be scary! Keep working at it and the speed will come.

SPONSORSHIPS

Professional mountain bikers earn money through sponsorships. This is when a company gives an athlete money or gear. The athlete **promotes** the company by wearing or using the gear. A mountain biker may ride a certain bike because they are sponsored by a company.

PUSHING THE LIMITS

An athlete may appear in ads or other **media** for a company as part of sponsorship too.

Even mountain bikers who have sponsorships may still have other jobs! At first, sponsorships may just cover the cost of gear or entrance fees for events. Those at the top of their game, however, get money as well!

PUSHING THE LIMITS

There are often prizes for those who win races too—money or biking gear usually.

Jolanda Neff

HOW TO GET PAID

One way to get a sponsor is to win! Once you compete well in a few larger events, it's likely a sponsor will be interested. You can also work to meet sponsors at events. Companies often have tents or tables selling their **merchandise**.

PUSHING THE LIMITS

Sometimes, you must earn enough points in smaller races to get into bigger races with other pros. Pay attention to the rules of each event!

You don't have to win—or even compete—to get a sponsor! Today, many mountain bikers and other athletes can earn money and gear through social media. When you are old enough, you can start a social media page just about your mountain-biking adventures.

PUSHING THE LIMITS

Posting exciting videos of your best runs and pictures of your best tricks can draw a big social media following. People with many followers can draw in sponsors.

You don't have to wait for a sponsor to come to you! Many pro mountain bikers reach out to companies and **brands** they want to work with. Be honest about who you are and what you want to accomplish. Tell them what's special about you!

PUSHING THE LIMITS

Even young riders can get sponsored! Their sponsors might just send parts for their bike or entrance fees for events, but that can grow as the rider does.

COMPETE AT HIGH LEVELS

Top pro mountain bikers keep working—even after they get paid to ride! There are many levels of competition to take part in as you get older. Some colleges have mountain-biking teams. There's even a World Cup for mountain biking!

PUSHING THE LIMITS

Pro mountain biker Becky Gardner says to get better, you have to ride what's hard for you: "A lot of people think doing the same thing over and over again is going to help them, but the problem is that they do things that are easy for them, over and over again."

AT THE OLYMPICS

Mountain biking became an Olympic sport in 1996. There are races for men and for women. In the event, the riders must do many laps around a mountainous, challenging trail. It usually takes a couple of hours and really tests riders' endurance.

PUSHING THE LIMITS

At the Tokyo Olympics held in 2021, Jolanda Neff won gold for the women and Thomas Pidcock won gold for the men.

Thomas Pidcock

HAVE FUN!

The number one thing professional mountain bikers tell young riders is to have fun! No matter how hard you work, try to enjoy it. It'll be easier to stick with it if you do. Now, go out there and ride!

PUSHING THE LIMITS

Remember: You don't have to compete or be a pro to try mountain biking! It's a challenging sport for friends and family to do together.

LEARN THE LINGO

bonk
when a mountain biker runs out of energy before the end of a race

endo
a crash during which a rider goes over the front handlebars

hard-tail
a kind of mountain bike that has front suspension, but not rear suspension

jump
a pickup in speed

kick
the last burst of speed when sprinting at the end of a race

neo-pro
the term used for a rookie, or new athlete, competing as a pro

soft-tail
a mountain bike with front suspension and rear suspension

FOR MORE INFORMATION

BOOKS

Gaertner, Meg. *Mountain Biking*. Mendota Heights, MN: Apex, 2022.

Hogan, Christa C. *Mountain Biking*. Minneapolis, MN: Abdo Publishing, 2020.

WEBSITES

Adventure Cycling Association

www.adventurecycling.org/routes-and-maps/adventure-cycling-route-network/

Check out maps and routes for all kinds of cycling here.

USA Cycling

usacycling.org/

Find out about USA Cycling, including racing for kids and mountain biking!

Publisher's note to educators and parents: Our editors have carefully reviewed these websites to ensure that they are suitable for students. Many websites change frequently, however, and we cannot guarantee that a site's future contents will continue to meet our high standards of quality and educational value. Be advised that students should be closely supervised whenever they access the internet.

GLOSSARY

brand: A group of products made by a company under a certain name.

compete: To try to win a contest with others. A competition is an event in which people try to win.

endurance: The power to do something hard for a long time.

experience: Awareness or skill gained from doing something.

media: The outlets and people that offer news coverage.

merchandise: Items being sold.

promote: To make people aware of.

suspension: A system of springs and other devices on a bike that reduces the shaking and bumping caused by uneven surfaces.

INDEX